ROBERT BURNS IN PERTHSHIRE

First published 2024
by Rymour Books
45 Needless Road,
PERTH
PH20LE

© Donald N M Paton 2024
ISBN 978-1-7394801-8-9

A CIP record for this book is
available from the British Library

Book and cover design by Ian Spring

Printed and bound by
Imprint Digital
Seychelles Farm
Upton Pyne
Exeter

All rights reserved. No part of this publication may be reproduced, stored in a retrieval system, or transmitted, in any form or by any means, electronic, mechanical, photocopying, recording or otherwise, without the prior permission of the publishers.

ROBERT BURNS IN PERTHSHIRE

Donald N M Paton

with a foreword by David Purdie

DEDICATION

To the many friends made over the years in my three Burns clubs – The Perth Burns Club, The Kinross Jolly Beggars and The Burns Club of Vancouver.

> "Still closer knit in Friendship's ties
> Each passing year".

ABOUT THE AUTHOR

DONALD N M PATON lives in Perth and spent most of his working life in advertising and publishing. A strong interest in the traditions and culture of Scotland and particularly the works of Robert Burns led to him becoming secretary of The Perth Burns Club, a position which he held for 35 years, including one year as president. He is now an honorary president of the club, a past president of The Burns Club of Vancouver and a former chieftain of the Kinross Jolly Beggars. In 2015, he was the recipient of the David K Thomson award for his services to cultural activity within Perth and Kinross. He is the author of three earlier books. His first, *Twixt Castle and Mart*, published in 2005, was a history of Perth's Needless Road, followed in 2014 by the anthology *Perth: As Others Saw Us* and in 2022 by *Nae Place Mair Braw*, a social history of the Craigie and Cherrybank area of Perth.

ACKNOWLEDGEMENTS

Whilst researching and writing this book, I inevitably had to draw on the work of a number of authors by taking notes on facts, quotations and opinions which appeared relevant to the purpose. I have tried to give full credit to these sources in the Bibliography but where I may have neglected to give full attribution, I offer my apologies to those concerned.

I am grateful to the National Trust Scotland and National Galleries Scotland for permission to reproduce images. Photographs that have not been credited have mainly been taken by myself or are from my personal collection. However, where I have been unable to trace the origin of a photograph, I again apologise for failing to acknowledge the source.

I am immensely grateful to Ian Spring of Rymour Books, for agreeing to take on the publication of the book, for designing the cover and for his expert guidance and professional advice. Thank you Ian – again you have made the magic happen and another dream come true!

I am deeply indebted to my good friend Professor David Purdie for taking time to write the Foreword to the book as there are few people who can match him in his knowledge of Scotland's national bard. David has long been regarded as one of the best after-dinner speakers both in the UK and internationally and I count myself as being extremely fortunate in having attended many Burns Nights in his company listening to his fine orations.

FOREWORD

Much has been written about Robert Burns's early days in Ayrshire and on his latter years in Dumfries. He was, however, a well-travelled poet and songwriter, not least to the fair city of Perth and its yet fairer countryside. Donald Paton's work in assembling Burns's links with this highly romantic part of Scotland is thus both welcome and long overdue.

The poet's connections with Perthshire began early. At the Edinburgh home of Professor Adam Ferguson, Perthshire-born at Logierait, the newly arrived Burns was presented to the apex of the capital's society, among them the economist Adam Smith and the young Walter Scott.

The county of Perth played a major role in the Bard's great project of both conserving and expanding Scotland's traditional song heritage. He set his immortal lyric *The Red, Red Rose* to the air *Major Graham of Inchbrackie,* the estate lying close to Crieff. His national anthem Robert Bruce's March to Bannockburn, popularly 'Scots wha hae…', was presented to General William Robertson of Lude, by Blair Atholl.

At Blair Castle came the poet's meeting with Josiah Walker who has left us our only first-hand description of Burns engaged in marrying words to airs collected on his Highland tour. It was also at Blair that the poet's future career as a civil servant was projected through his meeting with Robert Graham of Fintry, Commissioner of the Excise Service. To him Burns would later be indebted for protection from allegations of sedition.

The Journal of his Highland tour and his letters from a later visit to Sir William Murray at Ochtertyre provide us with a splendidly visual account of eighteenth-century social Scotland. Equally, its artistic side is highlighted by the account of his meeting at Dunkeld with Niel Gow, our greatest composer of fiddle music.

All in all, this book deploys the history, culture and the sheer visual beauty of Perthshire to illuminate the life and work of a great poet and songwriter at the peak of his powers. Read on!

                    Professor David W R Purdie, MD, FRCP Ed, FRSSA.
                          Co-editor, *The Burns Encyclopaedia.*

INTRODUCTION

In the late 1950s, at one of the first Burns Suppers I attended, I remember the proposer of the Immortal Memory stating that he had no knowledge of Robert Burns ever visiting Perth. There was little reaction to this — either because the bulk of the audience were not too well versed in the life of Burns and were only there for a good night out or, like myself, were totally oblivious to the fact that Scotland`s national bard had once spent a night in the Fair City despite the presence of a plaque above a High Street close giving details of his visit.

Perhaps this is understandable as, sadly, the poetry and life of Robert Burns was, in my day, given rather scant attention at primary and early secondary school. We got quite a lot of the English poets and writers such as Shakespeare, Wordsworth, Keats, Shelley and Milton but little of Burns and virtually nothing of Perth's own poet William Soutar. As a result, many Scottish people of my generation grew up without fully appreciating Scots language and the values that Burns set down as a great Scotsman. Considering that Scottish education was once recognised as being one of the best in the world that was, in my opinion, almost a crime.

I suppose I was rather fortunate in growing up in a Burns household. My father was in demand each year as a Burns speaker and I remember him going out on a cold January evening wearing his best suit to attend some local Burns Night. He was a fine Immortal Memorist and in the 'cold war' days of the early 1970s attended the first Burns Supper in Moscow which was open to guests from outside Russia.

Looking back, I think my first real interest in Robert Burns came as a fifteen-year-old Boy Scout when, along with fellow patrol leaders in the 53rd Perthshire Congregational Church Scout Troop and wearing a kilt borrowed from a neighbour, I was designated to be a haggis server at the church's annual Burns Supper. I remember enjoying the experience (it was my first taste of haggis) and being overawed by hearing someone recite the whole of *Tam o' Shanter* from memory and thinking 'I wish I could do that'! The wish was soon to be realised. In my later school years, I was fortunate in having an excellent teacher of English and I recall being encouraged to learn quotations from the works of Burns as there was generally a Burns question in the Highers. The seed planted at the church Burns Supper began to grow and shortly after leaving school I was back at that event reciting *Tam o`Shanter* and addressing the haggis at local Burns Nights (albeit with a book stuck in my pocket!).

When some years later I was invited to become a member of the Kinross Jolly Beggars Burns Club, I remember surveying what I considered was an elderly gathering and reflecting that the Burns tradition might soon die out. Fifty years on I am still attending that event — surveying another elderly gathering! When the Perth Burns Club was re-formed in 1977 after a lengthy spell in abeyance, I became the club secretary.

It was through my membership of these clubs and their connections with the Robert Burns World Federation that I began to develop a greater understanding of Burns's works by listening to a number of very well delivered and thoughtful Immortal Memories and hearing the sublime beauty of the songs. As a result, I found myself taking a deeper interest in the writings of Scotland's national bard. When attending a Burns Federation World Conference in Calgary, Canada in 1993 I met the lady who was to become my wife.

For many years I have been intrigued by the Highland tour undertaken by Robert Burns in 1787 and have sometimes felt that the connections the poet had with Perthshire, Kinross and Clackmannanshire during the late summer and autumn of that year were worthy of more detailed description and analysis. In many accounts, the Perthshire aspect of the tour is given only a brief mention and, although in reality Burns only spent a few days in the county, we should remember what he achieved in that short time in terms of preserving much of Scotland's almost forgotten traditional music and song.

We are familiar with some of the pieces from that visit to Perthshire such as *The Birks of Aberfeldy* or *Killiecrankie* and, over the years, countless people have viewed the verses which are on display in the Kenmore Hotel but how often do we read *The Humble Petition of Bruar Water, A Highland Welcome* or *Verses on Scaring Some Waterfowl at Glenturret*?

The journey undertaken by Robert Burns and his travelling companion William Nicol in September 1787 must not be underestimated. Travelling by a horse-drawn post-chaise, the popular mode of travel for eighteenth-century tourists, it must have been an arduous and exhausting trip over rough roads. Even in the early nineteenth century a journey from London to Edinburgh in a jolting stagecoach could take at least a week. Burns's later visit to Perthshire and Clackmannanshire in October of that same year was on horseback as were his tours of the West Highlands and the Borders. It has been estimated that the distance covered during the September tour of the Highlands was some six hundred miles, including all the windings and diversions. An amazing distance considering that it took Burns two days, including an overnight stop, to get from his Ayrshire home to Edinburgh. In the late eighteenth century many roads were tolled, involving delays, and were rough and unpaved. Burns wrote of this in *Epigram on Rough Roads*:

> I've now arrived — thanks to the gods —
> Thro' pathways rough and muddy,
> A certain sign that making roads
> Is no this people's study.

Altho' I'm no wi' Scripture cram'd
I'm sure the Bible says',
That heedless sinners shall be damn'd
Unless they mend their ways.

A few years ago I decided to retrace the steps of Burns's visit to Perthshire at exactly the same time of year taking photographs showing the area in its autumnal glory. The result of this was a powerpoint presentation which I have shown locally at various clubs and societies. It was after one of these meetings that someone suggested that I should consider putting the whole thing together in book form and this is the outcome.

As with his earlier Border tour, Burns kept a journal for his Highland tour of 1787 which has been published in facsimile and this was invaluable in my research. However, the journal often reflects the poet's hurry — being no more than staccato jottings or an itinerary and the unusual spelling of certain place names are his. The importance and literary content of the journal is of immense value as here we find Burns doing something that he really wanted to do, namely travel and allow his mind to become undisciplined from toil and just observe.

Burns was also a prolific letter writer and it is through reading the letters that one really gets a deeper insight into the nature and personality of the man. Fortunately, he wrote some of the letters during and just after his tour and they, along with his journals, make fascinating reading of eighteenth century Scottish rural and urban life, recreation and travel.

Pages from Burns's journal of 1787

I hope that this book will not only appeal to Burns enthusiasts but also to those who may be unaware of the wealth of Scottish music and song which was discovered and preserved for posterity in Perthshire and the surrounding area during a few days in 1787.

Donald N M Paton, FSA Scot
Perth, 2024

LIST OF ILLUSTRATIONS

Back cover:
Harvest fields at Lodierait
Plaque in Perth High Street
The Strathearn Valley

Robert Burns in Edinburgh	19
Peggy Chalmers	25
Roman camp at Ardoch	26
River Allan	28
River Earn at Comrie	28
Aberuchill Castle	29
Ossian's stone	30
The Sma' Glen	31
Loch Freuchie	31
Kenmore Hotel	32
Burns poem at Kenmore Hotel	34
Croft Moraig stone circle.	34
Loch Tay at Kenmore	35
Tay bridge at Kenmore	35
Falls of Acharn	36
Hermit's cave at Acharn	36
Glenlyon House	38
Castle Menzies	38
Birks of Aberfeldy	39
Birnam and Dunkeld from top of Birnam Hill	40
Trees on Birnam Hill	40
September fields at Logierait	41
River Braan at the Hermitage	41
The Hermitage	42

Sir Henry Raeburn's painting of Niel Gow	45
The pass of Killiecrankie	47
Blair Castle	48
The falls at Bruar	54
Old road at Dalnacaroch	56
Evelick Castle	59
The Carse of Gowrie	59
Plaque at Croom's Tavern	61
The grave of Bessie Bell and Mary Gray	63
The River May at Inveray	64
Harviestoun Castle	74
Ochtertyre House	64
Loch Turret	77
Euphemia Murray	77

CHAPTER ONE

Edinburgh and Preparing for the North

In 1787, Robert Burns was the wonder of Edinburgh. It was the time of the Scottish Enlightenment and Burns at twenty eight years old had become a part of it.

The first formal publication of his works, *Poems, Chiefly in the Scottish Dialect,* published in Kilmarnock in 1786 and paid for by subscription had changed Burns's life. It had taken him away from the grind of agriculture routine and made him a public figure. One of the six hundred and twelve copies of the Kilmarnock edition had reached Edinburgh where it was perceived to have some merit. Informed of this, Burns abandoned his plans for immigration to the West Indies – if indeed these plans had ever been all that serious – and left instead for Edinburgh on a borrowed pony to arrange for a new edition of his poems arriving there on 29th November 1786.

Burns was so fired up by this prospect of future success that, in his own words, he posted for that city, without a single acquaintance, or a single letter of introduction. His claim of not knowing anyone in Edinburgh is not quite accurate as he took up shared lodgings in Baxter's Close on the south side of the Lawnmarket with a friend, John Richmond, that he had known in Ayrshire. Baxter's Close has since been demolished but the approximate site of the house is Deacon Brodie's Tavern at the corner of Lawnmarket and Bank Street.

But Burns also had influential connections in Edinburgh whom he promptly approached on his arrival in the city. The first of these was Sir John Whiteford, erstwhile Master of St James Lodge, Tarbolton where Burns was Depute Master and another, again through his Masonic associations, was James Dalrymple. Dalrymple introduced Burns to James Cunningham, the 14th Earl of Glencairn who was a friend of the leading Edinburgh publisher William Creech and also a prominent member of the Caledonian Hunt, a select and gentrified field sports club. Through this new friendship with Lord Glencairn, Burns procured the support of the Caledonian Hunt as sponsors for one hundred copies of a new Edinburgh edition and set to work with the publisher William Creech.

If his sponsors, the Caledonian Hunt, represented the crème de la crème of the city then the Crochallan Fencibles (a gentlemen`s literary and convivial drinking club in which members took on assumed names and personae) represented the middle ranks of society where Burns felt more at home. He certainly appears to have been thoroughly at home in all-male society whether formal, as in the Tarbolton Bachelors' Club and the Crochallan Fencibles, or at informal gatherings where the male sharing of bawdy songs and stories cut across class lines. It is likely that many of the poems which make up *The Merry Muses* were presented by Burns at meetings of the Fencibles.

In the egalitarian howffs and clubs, Burns met sympathetic individuals some who were to become lifelong friends such as the metaphysician Professor Dugald Stewart and James Johnson, an engraver who was in the initial stages of a project to print all the tunes of Scotland in his *Scots Musical Museum*. The friendship with Johnson was to shift Burns's focus from poetry to song which was soon to become his principle creative form for the rest of his life.

As he made his way in Edinburgh society, Burns is alleged to have met on at least two occasions the infamous deacon, William Brodie, the respected citizen by day and thief by night, and the inspiration for Robert Louis Stevenson's novel *Dr Jekyll and Mr Hyde*.

Edinburgh at that time was in the hey-day of cultural nationalism and the works of Burns were being hailed as evidence of a Scottish culture with echoes of earlier written and oral Scottish literature. As a result, he was immediately taken up by the city`s literati and proclaimed to be a remarkable Scot.

Robert Burns was wined and dined by people who, almost without exception, were from a different class and background from him such as the Duchess of Gordon and the philosopher and historian Adam Ferguson, born at Logierait in Perthshire and at whose home he impressed (and was impressed by) a fifteen-year-old Walter Scott. Burns was regarded as the hit of the season and, although he knew full well what was going on, he intensified aspects of his rural persona to conform to expectations. He represented the creativity of the peasant Scot and, for a season, was Exhibit A for a distinct Scottish heritage.

The famous painting 'Robert Burns in Edinburgh, 1787' by Charles Martin Hardie ARSA, which depicts Burns reading his poem The Winter's Night at a literary gathering at the Duchess of Gordon`'s home in Edinburgh. (Courtesy of the National Trust for Scotland).

Whilst trying to prise royalties out of the miserly William Creech for the now highly successful Edinburgh edition of his poems, Burns was also finalising arrangements for his projected tours of Scotland. The tours had been in the poet's mind for some time for in a letter sent from his lodgings at the Lawnmarket on February 7th, 1787 to his would-be patron David Stewart Erskine, the eleventh Earl of Buchan, he wrote:

> Your Lordship touches the darling chord of my heart when you advise me to fire my muse at Scottish story and Scottish scenes – I wish for nothing more than to make a leisurely Pilgrimage through my native country; to sit and muse on those once hard-contended fields, where Caledonia, rejoicing, saw her bloody lion borne through broken ranks to victory and fame; and catching the inspiration, to pour the deathless Names in Song.

In March of that year he had further declared his wish when writing to a friend:

> Scottish scenes and Scottish story are themes I could wish to sing. I have no greater, no dearer aim, than to have it in my power, unplagu'd with the routine of business, for which Heaven knows I am unfit enough, to make leisurely pilgrimages through Caledonia; to sit on the fields of her battles; to wander on the romantic banks of her rivers; and to muse by the stately tower of venerable ruins, once the honored abodes of her heroes.

Two months later his pilgrimages had begun. In May he made a journey through the Borders and into the north of England. Towards the end of June he was in the West Highlands, described by him as a country where savage streams tumble over savage mountains, thinly overspread with savage flocks, which starvingly support as savage inhabitants.

A tour of the Highlands had been in the poet`s mind for some time. This trip, which was to become known as the Highland Tour, was planned with the intention of him meeting with some of his late father`s relatives in Kincardineshire but also to collect some of Scotland`s songs and tunes for publication in Johnson`s *Scots Musical Museum*.

Burns's choice of a travelling companion was his friend William Nicol, one of the classics masters of the High School of Edinburgh. It was an odd choice although it was a friendship that was to last throughout the poet`s lifetime. An acquaintance was to describe Nicol as a man of robust but clumsy person but added that Burns valued him on account of his vigorous talents, although they were clouded at times by coarseness of manners. Nicol has even been described as being a court jester, a tap-room philosopher, a crapulous and ill-natured ruffian. Another acquaintance who knew the two travellers noted that the same wit and power of conversation, the same fondness for convivial society and thoughtlessness of tomorrow, characterised both. Burns himself summoned up his fellow traveller in a phrase: 'His mind is like his body, he has a confounded strong in-knee'd sort of a soul'.

There were at least two occasions during their Highland tour when Burns had cause to regret his companion`s hasty temper and petty vanity. In retrospect, he referred to Nicol as 'that obstinate son of Latin prose,' while comparing himself during the excursion to a man travelling with a loaded blunderbuss at full cock! However, despite his failings, Nicol was undoubtedly a man of great talent and ability and it was probably his fondness of convivial relaxation which attracted Burns to him.

For his earlier tours in 1787, Burns had travelled on horse-back but for this trip to the north they decided to travel by post-chaise as, according to the poet, 'Nicol thinks it more comfortable than horse-back, to which I say, Amen.'

On the last Saturday of August 1787, a sound and serviceable chaise from Duncan MacCulloch in the Pleasance drew up at the Buccleuch Pend. Robert Burns and William Nicol packed their luggage into it and drove off over Edinburgh's North Bridge and along Princes Street, en route, by way of Corstorphine and Winchburgh, to Linlithgow.

But the post-chaise in which Burns set off on his Highland tour was also loaded with the unresolved problems of a troubled past (which included the relationship with Jean Armour who had birthed twins to him in September 1786) and the uncertainties of a doubtful future. His poems had now made him a national figure. His success in Edinburgh had gone ahead of him and he may also have seen this tour as a kind of triumphal procession.

He was the man of the moment but it is the nature of moments not to last. What would be waiting for him at the end of the tour?

CHAPTER TWO

Through Fertile Straths and Highland Grandeur

For the first two days the travellers rambled over the fertile carses of Falkirk and Stirling with Burns writing that they were delighted with the richly waving crops of wheat and barley.

They visited the Palace of Linlithgow, which inspired Burns to write the following words: 'what a poor pimping business is a Presbyterian place of worship; dirty narrow and squalid; stuck in a corner of old popish grandeur such as Linlithgow, and much more Melrose!'

James Cunningham, the fourteenth Earl of Glencairn, had given Burns a diamond stylus and, while at Stirling, he used it to write the following lines on the window pane of an inn to express his resentment and despair that the old royal palace had been allowed to fall into disrepair:

> Here Stewarts once in triumph reign'd,
> And laws for Scotland's weal ordain'd;
> But now unroof'd their Palace stands,
> Their sceptre's fall'n to other hands;
> Fallen indeed, and to the earth,
> Whence grovelling reptiles take their birth.
> The injur'd Stewart line are gone,
> A Race outlandish fill their throne;
> An idiot race to honour lost,
> Who knows them best despise them most.

These verses reflecting on the House of Hanover were to cause great offence, provoked many indignant comments and possibly rebounded on Burns during an early stage of the tour with the result that he smashed the window pane during a later visit to Stirling.

At Carron, near Falkirk, they were refused entry to the famous ironworks because it was a Sunday but Burns was thrilled to see the battlefield of Bannockburn of which he wrote:

> Here no Scot can pass uninterested. I fancy to myself that I see my gallant heroic countrymen coming o'er the hill and down upon the plunderers of their country, the murderers of their fathers; noble revenge and just hate glowing in every vein, striding more and more eagerly as they approach the oppressive, insulting, bloodthirsty foe! I see them meet in gloriously-triumphant congratulation on the victorious field, exulting in their heroic royal leader, and rescued liberty and independence.

On Sunday, August 26th, Burns and Nicol overnighted at Stirling and the following day Burns took a day away on his own to visit Harviestoun Castle near Dollar in Clackmannanshire, the home of the advocate John Tait.

> (Monday, 27 August) – go to Harvieston – Mrs Hamilton and family, Mrs Chalmers, Mrs Shields – go to see Cauldron Linn and rumbling bridge and deil's mill – return in the evening – supper – Messrs Doig, the Schoolmaster, Bell, and Captain Forrester of the Castle – D(oig), a queerish fellow and something of a pedant; B(ell) a joyous, vacant fellow, who sings a good song – Forrester, a merry, swearing kind of man, with a dash of the Sodger.

Burns had hoped that the visit to Harviestoun would be an opportunity for him to meet up with his special friend, Margaret (Peggy) Chalmers, whom he had first met back home in Ayrshire and then several times in Edinburgh at the home of Dr. Blacklock.

Peggy Chalmers

Although Margaret was not present at Harviestoun that Monday in August, her mother was there on a visit to Mrs Hamilton, the stepmother of Burns's friend in Ayrshire, Gavin Hamilton. John Tait of Harviestoun Castle was a widower whose deceased wife had been a sister of Mrs Chalmers and Mrs Hamilton and, after Tait's wife died, Mrs Hamilton and her family had moved to Harviestoun to become housekeepers at the castle.

If Burns regretted the absence of his friend Peggy Chalmers, it was more than made up by the presence of Mrs Hamilton's beautiful daughter, Charlotte, the younger half-sister of his friend Gavin. Burns accompanied Charlotte, Mrs Chalmers and other friends to local beauty spots on the River Devon and, although not over enthusiastic about the scenery, described that day in a letter to Gavin Hamilton as 'one of the most pleasant days I ever had in my life'. He was certainly captivated by the beauty of Charlotte who he referred to as 'the loveliest flower on the banks of the Devon who had once been a sweet bud on the braes of the Ayr'.

(Tuesday, 28 August) – morning – breakfast with Captain Forrester – Ochel Hills – Devon river – Forth and Tieth – Allan river – Strathallan – a fine country, but little improved – Ardoch camp – cross Earn of Crief – dine, and go to Aberuchil – cold reception at Aberuchil – a most romantically pleasant ride up Earn, by Auchtertyre and Comrie to Aberuchil – sup at Crieff.

The site of the Roman camp at Ardoch

Together again on the Tuesday morning, following the poet's solo visit to Harviestoun the previous day, Burns and Nicol left Stirling and made their way into Perthshire. At Ardoch, near Braco, they viewed the site of the Roman camp. As a Latin scholar, William Nicol was not only interested in the language but also in anything that pertained to the Romans. He knew all the historic sites which had been occupied by the Roman armies and had the chaise halted at Ardoch so that he could inspect the groundwork at that famous Roman camp.

Here, on the banks of the River Allan, Burns was inspired to later improve upon the words of an old song *Allan Water* which appears in his works as *By Allan Stream*. It is not only one of his finest songs but one of which he was justly proud and he wrote of it in a letter to George Thomson in 1793:

> I walked out yesterday evening with a copy of the Museum in my hand, when turning up Allan Water. It appeared to me rather unworthy of so fine an air; and recollecting that it is on your list, I sat and raved, under the shade of an old thorn, till I wrote one to suit the measure. I may be wrong, but I think it not in my worst

style. It is a good song. Should you think so too you can set the music to it and let the other follow as English verses. Autumn is my propitious season. I make more verses in it than all the year else.

> By Allan stream I chanc'd to rove,
> While Phebus sank beyond Ben Ledi;
> The winds were whispering thro' the grove,
> The yellow corn was waving ready.
> I listened to a lover's sang,
> And thought on youthfu' pleasures monie,
> And ay the wild-wood echoes rang:
> 'O, my love Annie's very bonnie!'

> O, happy be the woodbine bower,
> Nae nightly bogle makes it eerie!
> Nor ever sorrow stain the hour,
> The place and time I met my dearie!
> Her head upon my throbbing breast,
> She, sinking, said: 'I'm thine for ever!'
> While monie a kiss the seal imprest –
> The sacred vow we ne'er should sever.

> The haunt o' Spring's the primrose brae,
> The Summer joys the flocks to follow.
> How cheery thro' her shortening day
> Is Autumn in her weeds so yellow!
> But can they melt the glowing heart,
> Or chain the soul in speechless pleasure,
> Or thro' each nerve the rapture dart,
> Like meeting her, our bosom's treasure?

The River Allan

Their onward journey took them slowly through Strathallan, over the Muir of Orchill, through Muthill and across the River Earn to Crieff where they drew up at the door of old Gang Warily where they dined at their halting place for the day. In the afternoon, Burns, who had an introduction to Aberuchill House eight miles west along

The River Earn at Comrie

Aberuchill, where Burns received a cold reception.

Strathearn, set off in good spirits with Nicol. Although disappointed to learn at the Crieff inn that Sir William Murray of Ochtertyre House, was away from home, they decided to take the road that passed Ochtertyre since Burns was determined, since he could not visit Murray, to at least see his residence.

Burns wrote of a 'most romantically pleasant ride up the Earn, Auchtertyre and Comrie to Aberuchil'. However, Burns also wrote of having received a cold reception at Aberuchill and they quickly returned to Crieff where they had supper and spent the night.

It is highly likely that Burns was not made welcome at Aberuchill as a result of the verses which he had written earlier on the window pane in Stirling. Burns had hoped to visit Drummond Castle near Crieff during his tour but Captain Drummond, later Lord Perth, refused to entertain him. Drummond was a recent convert from Jacobitism and, having just got back the forfeited estates of his family, resented the verses on that account. Aberuchill House also belonged to the Drummonds!

> (Wednesday, 29 August) morning – leave Crieff – Glen Aumond – Aumond river – Ossian's grave – Loch Fruoch – Glenquaich – landlord and landlady remarkable characters – Taymouth – described in rhyme – Meet the hon. Charles Townsend.

The journey now took the pair through Glenalmond and the Sma' Glen. Here Burns viewed the alleged grave of Ossian which is marked by a large stone on the banks of the River Almond. Ossian was a reputed Gaelic bard of the 3rd century AD who may or may not have existed.

Whether he existed or not, he certainly did not write the words attributed to him. It was a James McPherson who invented romantic epics of the Celtic past and generously attributed them to Ossian. The genuineness of the stone in the Sma' Glen is more genuine than the works of Ossian but Burns stood by the stone and was moved by it. And his willingness to embrace a dream at the expense of the facts shouldn't surprise too many Scots.

James McPherson was to some extent a model for what many Scots have done with their history – he made emotional claims that can't be historically justified. Perhaps the unromantic reality of a country sold for money and the promise of jobs for the boys had created a guilt most easily compensated for by falsifying the facts. The irony of Burns paying homage there, was that he was the culmination of an alternative tradition and its most spectacular fulfillment – the incarnation almost of the great democratic tradition of Scottish literature.

Ossian's stone in the Sma' Glen .

The man who stood by Ossian's stone in the Sma' Glen in Perthshire that August morning in 1787 was the one living poetic voice strong enough to reassert powerfully the reality of Scottish history and blow away the myths of McPherson's Ossian.

At Amulree (where they found the landlord and landlady remarkable characters), Burns and Nicol turned sharply to their left and went up

The Sma' Glen .

Glen Quaich by the shores of Loch Freuchie where clans were armed and sworn in during the 1715 rising. Crossing over the one thousand seven hundred foot pass of Meall A'Choire Chreagaich, they then made the steep descent into Kenmore (then known as Taymouth) at the end of Loch Tay. At the Kenmore Inn they found comfort and rest. A chair, said to have been used by Burns during his visit, is now in Perth Art Gallery. They are likely to have dined well at Kenmore as R. L Willis when writing about Scotland's inns three years after Burns's visit in *A Tour from London to Elgin* stated:

Loch Freuchie in Glen Quaich

The cheapness of the inns is wonderful. We had today for dinner, fine fresh trout, a shoulder of mutton, two fowls and bacon, hung beef, and salmon salted, vegetables, cheese and an excellent bottle of port and the sum total was four shillings and twopence.

Ever prodigal of his occasional verses, it was here over the chimney-piece of the inn at Kenmore, at the outlet of Loch Tay, after a walk around the area, that Burns scribbled the lines on the whitewashed wall which are still preserved today and protected behind a sheet of glass. The verses are sometimes hailed as the Bard's best exercise in English heroics. Could he ever have imagined that these impromptu and delicate pencil marks would endure into the twenty-first century as evidence of his visit to Perthshire? Standing before that fireplace on a cold autumn afternoon and comforted by the heat of burning logs, it is not difficult to imagine Robert Burns occupying the same space and leaning against the wall to write the verses.

The 'hermit's mossy cell' mentioned in the poem, refers to the hermit's cave beside the Falls of Acharn. It was visited by Burns during his walk and can still be visited today if one is prepared to take the stiff climb up the hill from Acharn.

The palace to which Burns refers is Taymouth Castle which in 1787

Kenmore Hotel

was the seat of John Campbell (1762-1834), one of the sixteen Scottish representative peers. Campbell was created Baron Breadalbane of Taymouth Castle in 1806 and Marquis in 1831. Burns prefaced his *Address to Beezlebub* to Campbell.

Verses Written with a Pencil over the Chimney-piece in the Parlour of the Inn at Kenmore, Taymouth

Admiring Nature in her wildest grace,
These Northern scenes with weary feet I trace;
O'er many a winding dale and painful steep,
Th' abodes of coveyed grouse and timid sheep,
My savage journey, curious, I pursue,
Till fam'd Breadalbane opens to my view –
The meeting cliffs each deep-sunk glen divides,
The woods, wild-scattered, clothe their ample sides;
Th' outstretching lake, imbosomed 'mong the hills,
The eye with wonder and amazement fill;
The Tay meandering sweet in infant pride,
The palace rising on his verdant side;
The lawns wood-fringed in Nature's native taste;
The hillocks dropt in Nature's careless haste;
The arches striding o'er the new-born stream;
The village glittering in the noontide beam.
Poetic ardours in my bosom swell,
Lone wandering by the hermit's mossy cell;
The sweeping theatre of hanging woods,
Th' incessant roar of headlong tumbling floods.

(Thursday, 30 August) – come down Tay to Dunkeld – Glenlyon House – Lyon river – Druid's temple – 3 circles of stones – the outmost sunk

Verses transcribed over the chimneypiece at the Kenmore Hotel

– the 2nd has 18 stones remaining – the innermost has 8 – two detached ones like a gate, to the southeast – say prayers in it – Pass Tay bridge – Aberfeldy – described in rhyme – Castle Menzies – Grantully – Ballechin beyond – Loggierait – Inver – Dr Stewart – sup.

After the overnight stay at Kenmore, Burns and Nicol took time on the Thursday to sample some of the further glories of the area. They visited Glenlyon House, the seat of the Campbells of Glenlyon and occupied in Burns's day by Dr David Campbell; paused at Fortingall, an old capital of Gaelic culture; and stopped at what Burns called a Druid`s temple at the Croft Moraig stone circle beside

Croft Moraig stone circle

the River Lyon where Burns noted in his journal that he said prayers.

Continuing their journey they then visited Castle Menzies occupied by Sir John Menzies the Chief of the Clan Menzies, then passed through Weem and crossed over General Wade`s Bridge, completed in 1733 as part of the General's network of military roads, into Aberfeldy.

Loch Tay at Kenmore:
'Th' outstretching lake, imbosomed 'mong the hills'.

Bridge at Kenmore where the River Tay flows out of Loch Tay:
'The arches striding o'er the new-born stream'.

'Th' incessant roar of headlong tumbling floods' and 'the hermit's mossy cell' at the Falls of Acharn.

   The Birks of Aberfeldy is a wooded glen where, in certain places, a rocky ledge separates two banks of a mountain stream known as the Urlar Burn as it makes its way from the spectacular Falls of Moness towards the River Tay. It was here, whilst climbing the winding path of the steeply rising tree-covered slopes, that Burns wrote new words for an old tune and today a plaque in a slab of rock marks the spot where Burns is reputed to have composed these stanzas standing under the Falls of Moness:

>Now Simmer blinks on flowery braes,
>And o'er the chrystal streamlets plays;
>Come let us spend the lightsome days
>In the birks of Aberfeldy.

>The littlle birdies blythely sing
>While o'er their heads the hazels hing,
>Or lightly flit on wanton wing

In the birks of Aberfeldy.

The braes ascend like lofty wa's,
The foaming stream, deep-roaring fa's,
O'er hung with fragrant-spreading shaws,
The birks of Aberfeldy.

The hoary cliffs are crown'd wi' flowers,
White o'er the linns the burnie pours,
And, rising, weets wi' misty showers,
The birks of Aberfeldy.

Let Fortune's gifts at random flee,
They ne'er shall draw a wish frae me;
Supreme blest wi' love and thee
In the birks of Aberfeldy.

Bonie lassie, will ye go,
Will ye go, will ye go?
Bonie lassie, will ye go
To the birks of Aberfeldy?

Where James McPherson had seen a monumental landscape inhabited by improbable ants, Burns saw a landscape humanised by the everyday emotions of its people. And in that sense, The Birks of Aberfeldy is an important song – it shows the vision of Burns trying to connect with the real landscape of Scotland – not the misty imaginings of McPherson's Ossian. It also demonstrates the method that Burns would later use of taking an old tune, like an empty house, and re-peopling it with his own words – filling it with the laughter and grief of the present.

At the Birks of Aberfeldy, Burns came closest to the real destination of his Highland tour. Later, when he was ready, the old music would be waiting for him.

And he didn't have long to wait. It was waiting for him just a few miles down the River Tay at Inver, near Dunkeld.

Glenlyon House

(Friday, 31 August) – walk with Mrs Stewart and Beard to Birnam top – fine prospect down the Tay – Craigiebarns hills – hermitage on the Bran water, with a picture of Ossian – Breakfast with Dr Stewart – Niel Gow plays – a short, stout-built, honest highland figure, with his grayish hair shed on on his honest social brow – an interesting face, marking strong sense, kind open-heartedness mixed with unmistrusting simplicity – visit his house – Marget Gow.

Castle Menzies

After leaving Aberfeldy the previous day, the route had taken the travellers through Grandtully and Logierait to the hamlet of Inver where they were the overnight guests of Doctor Alexander Stewart who was a connection of Baroness Nairne through marriage and known as

~38~

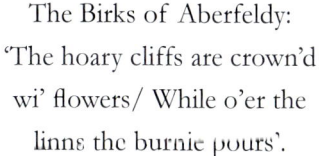

The Birks of Aberfeldy: 'The hoary cliffs are crown'd wi' flowers/ While o'er the linns the burnie pours'.

the Baron of Badenoch. He was also a close friend of the Duke of Atholl.

Before breakfast, Burns climbed to the top of Birnam Hill with Mrs Stewart and Beard. There is no mention of who Beard was and it is possible that this may have been a family retainer or perhaps a dog. He also visited the Hermitage on the River Braan with its picture of Ossian.

Following the energetic climb to the top of Birnam Hill and during breakfast at Inver with the Stewarts, Burns was introduced to Niel Gow, the famed Scots fiddler, who was then in his sixtieth year.

It was a most fortuitous meeting, for Burns was to draw many of the airs for his songs from Gow's dance tunes. Burns was also a fiddler and although not nearly as accomplished as Gow, he was good enough to acquire a few melodies which he later used for his songs. Gow's

A View of Dunkeld from the top of Birnam Hill

Trees on Birnam Hill

September Fields at Logierait

The River Braan

tune Major Graham of Inchbrakie was the air preferred by Burns for *My Love Is Like a Red, Red Rose*.

    Niel played a number of airs of his own composition and also

The Hermitage

some of the Bard's favourites such as *Tullochgorum*, *Invercauld Reel* and *Monymusk*. When Gow struck up *Locherrochside*, Burns is said to have expressed his delight and a wish to possess the air so that he might write verses to it. Gow complied with the request and the verses were written but it was another eight years before Burns sent them to George Thomson as *Address to the Woodlark*.

> O stay, sweet warbling woodlark, stay!
> Nor quit for me the trembling spray;
> A hapless lover courts thy lay
> Thy soothing fond complaining.
> Again, again that tender part
> That I may catch thy melting art!
> For surely that wad touch her heart,
> Wha kills me wi' disdaining.
>
> Say, was thy little mate unkind,

And heard thee as the careless wind?
Oh, nocht but love and sorrow joined
Sic notes o' woe could wauken!
Thou tells o' never ending care,
O speechless grief and dark despair –
For pity's sake, sweet bird, nae mair,
Or my poor heart is broken!

The song *Amang the Trees* in which Burns links Scotland's native music to the landscape was intended as a compliment to Gow.

Amang the trees, where humming bees
At buds and flowers were hinging, O,
Auld Caledon drew out her drone,
And to her pipe was singing, O.
'Twas Pibroch, Sang, Strathspeys and Reels -
She dirl'd them aff fu clearly, O,
When there cam a yell o foreign squeels,
That dang her tapsalteerie, O!

Their capon craws and queer 'ha, ha's,'
They made our lugs grow eerie, O.
The hungry bike did scrape and fyke,
Till we were wae and weary, O.
But a royal ghaist, wha ance was cas'd
A prisoner, aughteen year awa,
He fir'd a fiddler in the North,
That dang them tapsalteerie, O.

Local tradition has it that Burns and Gow repaired to the Inver Inn and on seeing and hearing an irate woman, Burns is said to have composed this impromptu verse although it is possible that he may have titivated it from an old Scots song:

> Ye gods, ye gave to me a wife,
> Out of your grace and pleasure.
> To be a partner of my life,
> And I was glad to have her.
> But if your providence divine,
> For better things design her,
> I obey your will at any time
> I'm willing to resign her.

A poem written by Burns to commemorate a later visit by Niel Gow to Dumfries is quoted on a plaque at Niel Gow's cottage at Inver.

> Nae fabled wizard's wand I trow,
> Had e'er the magic airt o' Gow,
> When wi' a wave he draws his bow,
> Across his wondrous fiddle.

Part of Niel Gow's success as Scotland's best fiddler lay in the fact that he had enjoyed the patronage of three Duke's of Atholl and, as Burns and Nicol then turned northwards up the River Tummel to Blair Atholl, the poet might well have wondered if that same patronage might be extended to himself. The omens were good as he had already received an invitation to meet the family. The journal entry for that day continues as follows:

Friday – ride up the Tummel river to Blair – Fascally, a beautiful romantic nest – wild grandeur of the pass of Killiecrankie – visit the gallant Dundee's stone. Blair – sup with the Duchess- easy and happy from the manners of the family – confirmed in my good opinion of my friend Walker.

Burns would certainly have been familiar with the account of the battle fought at Killiecrankie almost one hundred years earlier, on 27th July, 1689, between the Highlanders led by Viscount Dundee, James Graham of Claverhouse and the Anglo-Dutch troops commanded by General Hugh Mackay. By all the rules Burns should really have had little sympathy for Viscount Dundee who as Bluidy Clavers was alleged to have earlier caused much brutality against the Covenanters. However, as a general in the Scottish army, he had remained loyal to the Jacobite cause and this was how Burns now saw him. Not as a butcher of the rebel protesting Covenanters but as the Jacobite leader fighting gallantly for James and, at the moment of his victory over the enemy, falling mortally wounded.

To Burns, the stone that marked the spot where Dundee had fallen was symbolic of national defeat. But what nation was defeated? Was there indeed a Scottish nation in existence to suffer defeat or victory from an English nation?

Burns had a clear answer to these questions. Catholics, Protestants, Episcopalians (Dundee

Sir Henry Raeburn's painting of Niel Gow.

~45~

was a Scottish Episcopalian) and some of nondescript faiths had all joined together to fight for the Stewart cause. Had there been 'no alien race to fill the throne' he would have have been as contemptuous of the Stuarts as he was of the Hanoverians and the kith and kin of the 'Wee German Lairdie'. But a 'race outlandish' did now fill the throne and some forty years after the defeat of the Stuart cause at Culloden, Burns felt, as his ancestors had felt, that the Stuarts were still symbolic of Scotland as a nation and the defeat of the Stuarts had been the defeat of Scotland.

Thus, standing by that stone beside the River Garry in the Pass of Killiecrankie, Burns's imagination changed Graham of Claverhouse, the killer of Covenanters, into the gallant Lord Dundee – a symbol of the nation. Perhaps, it was here that the Bard of Ayrshire transcended his local boundaries and became the Bard of Scotland.

That visit to the Pass of Killiecrankie and the burial stone of Viscount Dundee was influential in Burns reworking the words of the old Jacobite song which was sung to the tune *An ye had been whare I hae been*. The teller of the tale is supposedly one of Mackay's men who was saved only by the deaths, in pursuit, of Haliburton of Pitcur and Claverhouse himself.

An ye had been whare I hae been,
Ye wad na been sae cantie, O!
An ye had seen what I hae seen,
On the braes o' Killiecrankie, O!

Whare hae ye been sae braw, lad?
Whare hae ye been sae brankie, O?
Whare hae ye been sae braw, lad?
Cam ye by Killiecrankie, O?

I faught at land, I fought at sea,
At hame I faught my auntie, O;
But I met the Devil and Dundee,
On the braes o' Killiecrankie, O.

The bauld Pitcur fell in a furr,
An Clavers gat a clankie, O.
Or I had fed an Athole gled,
On the braes o' Killiecrankie, O!

The Pass of Killiecrankie

The 'friend Walker' referred to in the journal entry was Josiah Walker, a man with Perth connections who ultimately became Professor of Humanity at Glasgow University and with whom Burns had become aquainted at the home of Dr Blacklock in Edinburgh. Walker had been appointed resident tutor to the Marquis of Tullibardine, the Duke of Atholl's eldest son who was then a boy of nine and in his Recollections of the Poet, he wrote:

On reaching Blair, he sent me notice of his arrival (as I had been previously acquainted with him) and I hastened to meet him at the inn. The Duke, to whom he brought a letter of introduction, was from home; but the Duchess, being informed of his arrival, gave him an invitation to sup and sleep at Athole House. He accepted the invitation; but as the hour of supper was at some distance, begged I would, in the interval, be his guide through the grounds. It was already growing dark; yet the softened though faint and uncertain view of their beauties, which the moonlight afforded us, seemed exactly suited to the state of his feeling at the time. I had often like others, experienced the pleasures which arise from the sublime or elegant landscape, but I never saw those feelings so intense as

Blair Castle

in Burns. When we reached a rustic hut on the River Tilt, where it is overhung by a woody precipice, from which there is a noble waterfall, he threw himself on the heathy seat and gave himself up to a tender, abstracted and voluptuous enthusiasm of imagination. I cannot help thinking it might have been here that he conceived the idea of the following lines which he afterwards introduced into his poem on Benny Water, when only fancying such a combination of objects as were now present to his eye:

> Or by the reaper's nightly beam
> Mild, chequering through the trees,
> Rave to my darkly – dashing stream,
> Hoarse – swelling on the breeze.

It was with much difficulty I prevailed on him to quit this spot, and to be introduced in proper time to supper.

Unlike his earlier dismissal of the scenery on the River Devon, Burns certainly appears to have been captivated by the scenery during this part of his tour. Perhaps not having the distraction of a bonnie lassie helped!

Walker was also greatly anxious to see how the poet would conduct himself in high society – 'in company so different to what he had been accustomed to' and later wrote:

> His manner was unembarrassed, plain and firm. He appeared to have complete reliance on his own native good sense for directing his behaviour. He seemed at once to perceive and to appreciate what was due to the company and to himself, and never to forget a proper respect for the separate species of dignity belonging to each. He did not arrogate conversation, but when led into it, he spoke with ease, propriety and manliness. He tried to exert his abilities, because he knew it was ability alonegave him a title to be there. The Duke's fine young family attracted much of his admiration; he drank their healths as 'honest men and bonnie lassies', an idea which was much appreciated by the company and with which he has very felicitously closed his poem. (The poem referred to by Walker is *The Humble Petition of Bruar Water*).

(Saturday, September 1) – visit the scenes round Blair – fine, but spoilt with bad taste – Tilt and Garry rivers – falls on the Tilt – heather seat – ride in company with Sir William Murray and Mr Walker to Loch Tummel – meanderings of the (Tummel), which runs through quondam Struan-Robertson's estate from Loch Rannoch to Loch Tummel – Dine at Blair – Company – General Murray, rien – Captain Murray, an honest Tar – Sir W. Murray, an honest, worthy man, but tormented with the hypochondria – Mrs Graham, belle et amiable – Miss Cathcart – Mrs Murray, a painter – Mrs King – Duchess and fine family, the Marquis, Lords James, Edward and Robert – Ladies Charlotte, Amelia and (Elizabeth) – children dance – sup – Duke – Mr Graham of Fintray – Mr

McLaggan, Mr and Mrs Stewart.

The above journal entry gives a clear description of the day spent exploring the countryside around Blair Atholl although some of the comments would appear to relate to the previous evening spent with Josiah Walker beside the River Tilt. It is interesting to note that Burns spent much of the day in the company of Sir William Murray of Ochtertyre whom he had tried to meet a few days earlier when at Crieff.

The two days that Robert Burns spent at Blair were later declared by him to have been among the happiest days of his life. Indeed if it had not been for the fretful impatience of William Nicol, his travelling companion, he would have prolonged his stay. Nicol became angry that Burns had stayed here so long and demanded that they leave, otherwise he would go on alone. Nicol was a kind of troublesome conscience for Burns reminding him of who he really was. Burns obeyed the promptings but was annoyed at the hasty departure although he might have been less annoyed if he had understood more fully the Duke`s reasons for wanting him to stay.

When Burns met the Duke on the second day of his visit he was informed that the uncrowned king of Scotland Henry Dundas, the political lieutenant in Scotland of William Pitt and president of the Board of Control was expected at Blair Castle as a guest.

Josiah Walker, in a letter to Burns dated 13th September 1787, wrote:

You know how anxious the Duke was to have another day of you, and to let Mr Dundas have the pleasure of your conversation as the best dainty with which he could entertain an honoured guest.

It would appear that, even in those days, a place like Blair Castle charged a price for admission for people like Burns. It was what you might call a tax on personal pride. Perhaps a part payment of that tax was *The Humble Petition of Bruar Water*.

When it became clear to the Duke that the travellers would be leaving on the Sunday morning, he advised the poet not to miss the Falls of Bruar on his journey north. Walker suggested that Burns could repay the hospitality he had received by writing some descriptive verses on any of the scenes with he had been so much delighted.

Advice and suggestion were both acceptable and, three days later, Burns wrote the following letter to Walker from Inverness on 5th September enclosing *The Humble Petition of Bruar Water to the Noble Duke of Athole*:

> I have just time to write the foregoing, and to tell you that it was (at least part of it) the effusion of an half-hour I spent at Bruar. I do not mean it was extempore, for I have endeavoured to brush it up as well as Mr Nicol's chat and the jogging of the chaise would allow. It eases my heart a good deal, as rhyme is the coin with which a poet pays his debts of honor or gratitude. I shall never forget the fine family piece I saw at Blair; the amiable, the truly noble Duchess, with her little seraph in her lap, at the head of the table; the lovely olive plants, as the Hebrew bard finely says, round the happy mother; the beautiful Mrs Graham; the lovely, sweet Miss Cathcart. (Catherine Charlotte), &c. I wish I had the powers of Guido to do them justice. My lord Duke's kind hospitality – markedly kind indeed. Mr Graham of Fintray's charms of conversation; Sir W. Murray's friendship; in short, the recollection of all that polite, agreeable company raises an honest glow in my bosom.

The meeting with Robert Graham of Fintry in Stirlingshire had a particularly positive outcome for Burns as it was through him that he later obtained employment in Dumfries as an exciseman

The Miss Cathcart and the Mrs Graham, whose praises Burns sings, were sisters of the Duchess of Atholl and all three, as it happened, were to die before even the short-lived poet. The beautiful Mrs Graham was married to the quiet Perthshire laird, Thomas Graham of Balgowan, who later, in middle life, volunteered as a soldier when the war with France broke out. He commanded the British troops at Barossa in 1811 and was thereafter created Lord Lynedoch. His name and title and the places with which he was associated are commemorated in several of Perth's street names and by the Lynedoch obelisk on Murrayshall Hill near Scone.

The Cathcarts were disappointed to hear that Burns and Nicol were about to leave Blair to continue their journey north. So anxious were they to have at least a few hours longer of Burns's company that they conspired a plot to delay their departure and which was described in detail in Josiah Walker's letter of 13th September:

> You know likewise the the eagerness the ladies shewed to detain you; but perhaps you do not know the scheme they devised, with their usual fertility in resources. One of the servants was sent to your driver to bribe him to loosen or pull off a shoe from one of his horses, but the scheme failed. The driver was incorruptible.

As to *The Humble Petition of Bruar Water*, it was written in the form of a plea from the River Bruar itself to the Duke of Atholl to take away the bareness of the area by planting trees.

> My lord, I know, your noble ear
> Woe ne'er assails in vain;
> Embolden'd thus, I beg you'll hear
> Your humble slave complain,

How saucy Phebus' scorching beams,
In flaming summer-pride,
Dry-withering, waste my foamy streams,
And drink my crystal tide.
Here, foaming down the skelvy rocks,
In twisting strength I rin;
There high my boiling torrent smokes,
Wild-roaring o'er a linn;
Enjoying large each spring and well,
As Nature gave them me,
I am, altho' I say it mysel,
Worth gaun a mile to see.
Would, then, my noble master please
To grant my highest wishes,
He'll shade my banks wi' tow'ring trees
And bonie spreading bushes.
Delighted doubly then, my lord,
You'll wander on my banks,
And to listen monie a grateful bird
Return you tuneful thanks.
Let lofty firs and ashes cool,
My lowly banks o'erspread,
And view, deep-bending in the pool,
Their shadows' wat'ry bed:
Let fragrant birks, in woodbines drest,
My craggy cliffs adorn,
And, for the little songster's nest,
The close embow'ring thorn!
So may, Old Scotia's darling hope,
Your little angel band
Spring, like their fathers, up to prop

Their honoured native land!
So may, thro' Albion's farthest ken,
To social-flowing glasses
The grace be – 'Athole's honest men,
And Athole's bonnie lasses!'

Although not particularly interesting in itself, the poem does offer an interesting subtext suggestive of the division in Burns between his natural pride and his position of dependency on the hospitality of the wealthy. He was perhaps realising that success and acceptance had a price, part of which involved compromising the broadness of his voice, though his native accent could never be entirely stifled.

It may be that the comfort and sociability of Blair Atholl and the idyll of Bruar Water were with him for some time as he travelled, replacing the harsher reality of contemporary Scotland with a surplus pleasantness.

The Falls of Bruar: 'Here, foaming down the skelvy rocks, in twisting strength I rin,.

The poem was certainly well accepted at Blair Castle as Josiah Walker continued to write in his letter:

Your verses have given us much delight, and I think will produce their proper effect. They produced a powerful one immediately; for the morning after I read them, we all set in procession to the Bruar, where none of the ladies had been these seven or eight years, and again enjoyed them there.

It only remains to be recorded that the noble Duke acceded to the humble petition and that trees were thickly planted along the chasm. One biographer of Burns has suggested that this was the only wish which the poet ever uttered that any pains were taken to gratify.

The Falls of Bruar, just north of Blair Atholl, are now one of Perthshire's most popular beauty spots and what makes the place so spectacular is the simple combination of rock, water and trees which offers grandeur on a magnificent scale. At the foot of a deep gorge the Bruar Water roars over a series of falls and cascades before surging through an arch into the pools below.

Since the planting of the first trees by the Duke of Atholl in 1797 in response to Burns's plea, further generations of Dukes of Atholl have planted trees in and around the area putting the woodlands of Atholl amongst the best wooded areas of the Highlands.

There is no doubt that Robert Burns was responsible for changing the character of the Falls of Bruar and one wonders what the Atholl area would be like today if the poet had not felt the need to advise the eighteenth century laird on how to improve his property.

An instance perhaps of the power of simple verse changing both attitudes and an entire landscape.

> (Sunday, 2 September) – Come up the Garrie – falls of Bruar – Daldecairoch – Dalwhinnie – dine – snow on the hills 17 feet deep – no corn from From Loch Garrie to Dalwhinnie – Cross the Spey and come down stream to Pitnim – Straths rich – les environs picturesque – Craigiow hill – Ruthven of Badenoch – barracks – wild and magnificent – Rothiemurchie on the other side, and Glenmore – Grant of Rothiemurchie's poetry told me by the Duke

of Gordon – Strathspey rich and romantic.

After leaving Blair and visiting the Falls of Bruar, Burns and Nicol crossed the county's northern boundary and, as they travelled up the River Garry to Dalnacardoch and into Inverness-shire, the hospitality of the previous two days must still have been uppermost in the poet's mind when he wrote the words to *A Highland Welcome*:

When Death's dark stream I ferry o'er
(A time that surely shall come)
In Heaven itself I`ll ask no more,
Than just a Highland welcome.

The old Highland road at Dalnacaroch

Across the Perthshire/Inverness-shire border at Dalwhinnie, Burns noted that there was snow on the hills seventeen feet deep. They visited the ruined Ruthven Barracks and Aviemore before continuing northwards.

While in the north, their journey took them to Inverness, Culloden, Forres, Fochabers, Elgin, Banff, Peterhead and Aberdeen before Burns finally met some of his relations in Stonehaven, Laurencekirk and Montrose. Thereafter they travelled by Arbroath and overnighted in Dundee before again returning to Perthshire.

This first part of the tour was to leave a lasting impression on Burns prompting him to later write words for this song to the tune of *Failte na miosg* – the first verse and refrain is traditional but the other verses are Burns's own composition:

My heart`s in the Highlands, my heart is not here
My heart`s in the Highlands, a-chasing the deer.
A-chasing the wild deer, and following the roe –
My heart`s in the Highlands, wherever I go!

Farewell to the Highlands, farewell to the North,
The birthplace of valour, the country of worth!
Wherever I wander, wherever I rove,
The hills of the Highlands for ever I love.

Farewell to the mountains, high-covered with snow,
Farewell to the straths and green valleys below.
Farewell to the forests and wild-hanging woods,
Farewell to the torrents and loud-pouring floods!
The hills of the Highlands for ever I love.

CHAPTER THREE

A Night in Perth and the Homeward Journey

(Friday, 14 September) – breakfast with the Miss Scots – Mr Mitchel and honest Clergyman – Mr Bruce another, but pleasant, agreeable and engaging – The first from Aberlemno – the second from Forfar – dine with Mr Anderson, a brother-in-law of Miss Scots – Miss Bess Scot like Mrs Greenfield – my bardship almost in love with her – come thro' the rich harvests and fine hedge rows of the carse of Gowrie, along the romantic margin of the Grampian Hills, to Perth – Castle – Huntly – Sir Stewart Threipland.

Following an overnight stay in Dundee, the route to Perth would actually have been by the foothills of the Sidlaw Hills (not the Grampians as described by Burns) and along the old carse road the high or braes road passing through Kinnaird and Fingask. It would have taken them up the Washinghouse Brae from Glencarse and into Perth by way of Corsiehill (where Burns took note of the fine view) then across the River Tay over the Perth Bridge, completed only sixteen years earlier in 1771 by John Smeaton.

The mention in the journal of Sir Stewart Threipland would suggest that Burns and Nicol may have paid a visit to Fingask House, near Rait. Sir Stewart Threipland (1716-1805) was a fervent Jacobite who had had been an ardent adherent of Prince Charles Edward Stuart throughout the entire Jacobite rebellion of 1745 and his older brother, David, had been killed at the battle of Prestonpans. After surviving the battle at Culloden in 1746, Sir Stewart, after innumerable adventures with Prince Charles, had fled to France disguised as a bookseller's assistant while Fingask was plundered by dragoons who destroyed everything which seemed of value, including the bed in

The Carse of Gowrie

which the Chevalier had slept during two visits to Fingask in 1716. After returning from France, Sir Stewart practised as a physician in Edinburgh and in 1766 had been President of the Royal College of Physicians of Edinburgh. He prospered sufficiently to buy back Fingask for £12,207

The ruined Evelick Castle

in 1783 and the baronetcy was restored to his son, Sir Patrick in 1826. A meeting with Sir Stewart, not long after paying homage to Viscount Dundee at Killiecrankie, would surely have appealed to Burns.

While on this journey through the Carse of Gowrie (described in Burns's later song *Yon Wild Mossy Mountains* as 'Gowrie's rich valley'), they would also have passed close to Evelick Castle, the ancient home of the Lindsay family and the scene of the romantic story of Elizabeth Lindsay and her Highland lover. Burns collected a fragment of the song during his tour which he sent to Johnson for the *Scots Musical Museum*. The complete ballad, which became a popular song, was not published until 1806 – ten years after the death of Burns.

> Will ye go to the Highlands, Leezie Lindsay,
> Will ye go to the Highlands wi' me?
> Will ye go to the Highlands, Leezie Lindsay,
> My pride and my darling to be?

We wish that Burns had told us more about his one night in Perth. However, we know that he stayed at Croom's Tavern in the High Street with the proprietors Mr and Mrs Croom, the parents of the Rev David Murray Croom (1810-1882) of Lauriston Place Church, Edinburgh. The Perth Crooms knew all about their distinguished guest as the Ayrshire poet and satirist who had astonished the big folk in Auld Reekie by his strapping figure, his noble head, his dazzling black eyes and his matchless conversation. It has been said that when Burns stopped at an inn for the night during his tours, the servants would get out of bed just to listen to him talk!

Burns is reputed to have consumed a baker's dozen of Perth pies washed down with draughts of mild porter but the Crooms remarked that, unlike William Nicol, he tasted nothing stronger. Croom, the Perth vintner, noted and subsequently, when in his later years, told his clerical son that Nicol looked sulky, seldom spoke and appeared annoyed at the free and full rush of language from Burns`s lips as he dilated upon the Tay, the view from Perth Bridge of the North Inch with the hills beyond and other subjects. The Crooms remembered that Burns`s table talk seemed altogether extraordinary in its strength, insight, humour and range.

One would prize a recording of Robert Burns during that one-night stay at the High Street tavern. So keen a critic as Principal Robertson who knew and conversed with Tobias Smollett, Adam Smith, David Hume and many other eminent men and women, has said that the conversation of Robert Burns was even more wonderful than any of his poems that autumnal evening at Croom's change house when the

> ROBERT BURNS VISITED PERTH
> 14TH–15TH SEPT 1787 AND
> STAYED AT CROOM'S TAVERN
> HIGH STREET.
> BUILDING IN CLOSE — LEFT-HAND SIDE

Burns plaque at the site of Croom's Tavern, Perth High Street

candles were brought forth and the night was fairly setting in.

Burns was the magnetic centre of attraction. They listened to the young man, eloquent, shedding his prophetic soul in melodious speed as if spell-bound. It was, as Croom affirmed, a most superior occasion, a rich intellectual treat edifying and stimulating the listeners. To see so true a man and poet as Robert Burns and to hear him talk with snatches of human portraiture of the men and women he had met on the wide stage of life, speaking with energy, his glowing eyes flashing round the circle of eager and intent admirers, was worth much to these eighteenth century Perth citizens.

The minister of Lauriston Parish church was proud, as were also his distinguished sons – Professor Sir John Halliday Croom (1847-1923) of Edinburgh University and The Rev David Brown Croom (1851-1913) of St Luke's Church, Montrose – to learn of Robert Burns being for one classic night in their relative's modest but cosy Perth hostelry. The memory of it recalled innocent glee, sparkling swift wit, winsome humour, candour and untrammelled sense.

Today, the site of Croom's Tavern is marked by a bronze plaque above the doorway at 186 High Street and was restored in 1992 by The Perth Burns Club – a club which was instituted in 1873, less than one hundred years after the poet`s only visit to the Fair City.

(Saturday, 15 September) – Perth – Scoon – picture of the Chevalier and his sister – Queen Mary's bed, the hangings wrought with her own hands – a fine, fruitful, hilly, wooded country round Perth – Taybridge – Mr and Mrs Hastings – Major Scott – Castle Gowrie. Leave Perth, Saturday morn – come up Strathearn to Endermay to dine – fine fruitful cultivated Strath – the scene of Bessy Bell and Mary Gray near Perth – fine scenery on the banks of the May – Mrs Belches, gawcie, frank, affable, fond of rural sports, hunting, etc – Miss Stirling her sister, enverite – come to Kinross to lie – Reflections in a fit of the colic.

Although mentioned in Burns's journal entry for September 15, it is not clear if the visit to Scone Palace happened on that day or the previous one. Scone Palace is situated on the east bank of the River Tay and would have been clearly visible to the travellers as they descended into Perth from Corsiehill. It certainly would have been easy for them to make a slight detour to the palace and then retrace their steps to enter Perth itself over Smeaton's Bridge. The fact that Burns also mentions Mr and Mrs Hastings and Major Scott in his journal (before he mentions leaving Perth) would suggest that he met these people on the Friday evening when staying at Croom's Tavern. The Hastings were members of the merchant family of Hastings of Perth and Major Scott was the brother of David Scott of that same family. The Castle Gowrie to which Burns refers was the Gowrie House, the scene of the mysterious plot against King James VI and I known as the Gowrie Conspiracy.

The mention of Bessie Bell and Mary Gray in the journal entry is interesting as Burns would not have had time to actually visit their grave at the Dronach Haugh on the banks of the River Almond and still reach Invermay in time for lunch. It is more likely that, while he was guesting at Blair Atholl, he was told the story of the two Perth maidens who built themselves a riverside bower to escape the 1645 plague but, unfortunately, were visited by a young man from plague-stricken Perth and, as a result, caught the infection and died. He may also have been familiar with the old ballad which relates:

> They thought to lie in Methven Kirk
> Among their noble kin
> But they maun lie on Lynedoch brae
> To beek fornent the sun.
> O Bessie Bell and Mary Gray
> They were twa bonnie lassies
> They biggit a bower on yon burn-brae
> And theekit it o'er wi' rashes.

It was possibly Mrs Graham of Balgowan who Burns met at Blair and on whose estate the grave was (and still is) situated who related the tale and perhaps the old ballad to Burns for the aforementioned letter from Josiah Walker contained the following passage:

> When you pay your promised visit to the Braes of Ochtertyre, Mr and Mrs Graham of Balgowan beg to have the pleasure of conducting you to the bower graves of Bessie Bell and Mary Gray.

The grave of Bessie Bell and Mary Gray

Certainly, the tale of the two unfortunate girls must have left a lasting impression on the poet for him to give it a mention in his journal and although Burns did pay the promised visit to

Ochtertyre later in the year, there is no evidence that he managed to include a visit to the Grahams at Balgowan.

At Invermay House near Forteviot he lunched with the Belches family who, a few years after Burns's visit, were to become connected with another of Scotland's great literary figures when Wilhelmina Belches had a romantic liason with Sir Walter Scott. Indeed, Scott (who was a fifteen year old boy when Burns met him in Edinburgh) would be a regular visitor at Invermay where a bridge over the picturesque little River May is known as Scott's Bridge.

Ochtertyre House

The River May at Invermay

Burns was certainly impressed by the fine scenery on the banks of the May and would have been familiar with the old song *The Birks of Invermay or Shades of Endermay* which was the favourite song of the Edinburgh poet Robert Ferguson (1750-1774) and reputedly sung by Ferguson as he was dying. Several sets of lyrics have been written to the old tune but the original two stanzas are thought to have been by William Malloch or Mallet (1714-1765). Later verses of the song are attributed to the Rev Alex Bryce (1713-1786) the minister at Kirknewton.

> The smiling morn, the breathing spring,
> Invite the tuneful birds to sing,
> And while they warble from each spray,
> Love melts the universal lay;
> Let us, Amanda, timely wise,
> Like them improve the hour that flies,
> And in soft raptures waste the day,
> Among the birks of Invermay.
> For soon the winter of the year,
> And age, life's winter, will appear;
> At this thy living loom will fade,
> As that will strip the verdant shade;
> Our taste of pleasure then is o'er,
> The feather'd songsters are no more;
> And when they droop, and we decay,
> Adieu the birks of Invermay.

From a personal point of view it is interesting to note that two of the people Burns and Nicol lunched with at Invermay House and referred to in that journal entry, were ancestors of mine. Mrs Belches and her sister Miss Stirling were of the Stirlings of Keir House near Dunblane and my great-grandmother on my mother's side, Eliza Stirling and my great-aunt Ann Stirling, were from that same family. During the Second World War it was another Stirling from Keir House, Sir David Stirling, who formed the SAS.

Continuing their southward journey, Burns and Nicol left Invermay and would have travelled over the Ochil Hills by way of the old Wallace Road to Glenfarg (then known as Damhead) and on to Kinross where they spent the night. Burns wrote in his journal that he had reflections in a fit of the colic at Kinross but perhaps these serious reflections had more bearing on his far past than on this recent journey which appears to have been a journey of unmingled and innocent gratification.

Although not commented upon, it is entirely likely that, while at Kinross, Burns would have viewed Loch Leven and the castle on the island where Mary Queen of Scots was imprisoned. It is also believed that while in the area he picked up the words and pipe tune of a traditional Fife song *Hey ca' thro'* which he reworked in 1792

> Up wi'the carls of Dysart.
> And the lads o' Buckhiven,
> And the Kimmers o' Largo,
> And the lasses o' Leven.
> Hey ca' thro' ca' thro'
> For we hae mickle a do,
> Hey ca' thro' ca' thro'
> For we hae mickle a do,
>
> We hae tales to tell,
> And we hae sangs to sing;
> We hae pennies to spend,
> And we hae pints to bring.
> Hey ca' thro' &c.
>
> We'll live a' our days,
> And them that come behin'
> Let them do the like,
> And spend the gear they win.
> Hey ca' thro' &c.

The town of Kinross still has a close connection with Robert Burns. In 1888, Robert Burns Begg (1833-1900), a great-nephew of the poet and the grandson of his youngest sister Isabella (1771-1858), was sheriff clerk of Kinross-shire and founded the Kinross Jolly Beggars Burns Club. Apart from imposed breaks caused by the First and Second World Wars and more recently by the Covid pandemic this well-attended gathering has taken place every January since its formation.

(Sunday, 16 September) – come through a cold barren country to Queensferry – dine – cross the Ferry and come to Edinburgh.

That final entry in the poet's journal of the Highland tour is so brief that one can almost sense his fatigue.

It had been an exacting tour of twenty two days but Robert Burns returned to Edinburgh with a heart steeped in wit, pathos and melody and, most importantly, with a collection of Scotland's almost forgotten traditional music. In a letter he wrote: My journey through the Highlands was perfectly inspiring; and I hope I have laid in a good stock of new poetical ideas from it.

On the day after his return to Edinburgh, Burns wrote to his brother Gilbert:

I arrived here safe yesterday evening after a tour of 22 days, and travelling over 600 miles; winding included. My farthest stretch was about 10 miles beyond Inverness. I went through the heart of the Highlands by Crieff, Taymouth the famous seat of Lord Breadalbane, down the Tay, among cascades & Druidical circles of stones, to Dunkeld seat of the Duke of Athole, thence across Tay and up one of his tributary streams to Blair of Athole another of the Duke's seats, where I had the honour of spending nearly two days with his Grace and Family, thence many miles through a wild country among cliffs grey with eternal snows and gloomy, savage glens till I crossed Spey and went down the stream through

Strathspey so famous in Scottish Music, Badenoch, &c. till I reached Grant Castle, where I spent half a day with Sir James Grant and Family, then cross the country for Fort George – call by the way at Cawdor the ancient seat of McBeth you know in Shakespear, there I saw the identical bed in which Tradition says king Duncan was murdered, lastly from Fort George to Inverness.

I returned by the coast: Nairn, Forres, and so on to Aberdeen, thence to Stonehive where James Burness from Montrose met me by appointment. I spent two days among our relatives, and found our aunts, Jean and Isbal still alive and hale old women, John Caird, though born the same year as our father, walks as vigorously as I can; they have had several letters from his son in New York. William Brand is likewise a stout old fellow; but further particulars I delay till I see you, which will be in two or three weeks.

The rest of my stages are not worth rehearsing – warm as I was from Ossian's country where I had seen his very grave, what cared I for fisher-towns and fertile carses? I slept at the famous Brodie of Brodie's one night and dined at Gordon castle next day with the Duke, Duchess and family.

Now back in Edinburgh, Burns turned once more to the business of earning a living. He toyed for a while with the two opportunities which had presented themselves to him – the development of his farming interests or to join the Excise as an officer, possibly following a suggestion made to him at Blair Castle by Robert Graham of Fintry. His mind was also still occupied with the task of getting William Creech, his publisher, to settle his business as, in a letter to Patrick Miller, he wrote: 'I am determined not to leave Edinr till I wind up my matters with Mr Creech, which I am afraid will be a tedious business.'

By this time, Burns's relations with Creech were no longer cordial and the poet wrote of him as:

A little upright, pert, tart, tripping wight,
And still his precious self his dear delight;
Who loves his own smart shadow in the streets
Better than e'er the fairest She he meets.
His meddling vanity, a busy fiend,
Still making work his selfish craft must mend.

Impatient, after two weeks of waiting in Edinburgh and with the happy memory of the Highland tour still in his mind, in early October Burns set out on another round of visits – this time in the company of Dr James McKittrick Adair, the son of an Ayr doctor. Although described as a headstrong, roving man who was always off to a new start but never winning through, Adair was probably a more genial travelling companion than William Nicol.

This trip, although intended as a tour of Stirlingshire and Clackmannanshire, was to take him back into Perthshire — but this time with romance on his mind.

CHAPTER FOUR

Sparks of Celestial Fire

Burns and Adair's destination on this new trip was Harviestoun Castle where Burns had gone for a day on his own during the early part of his tour with Nicol.

Still with fond memories of that brief visit in late August and with the knowledge that this time Margaret Chalmers and her cousin Charlotte Hamilton would both be present, it would have been with a happy heart and perhaps a preconceived plan that Burns returned to Harviestoun.

Burns's relationship with these two girls is a complicated one to work out but there is no doubt from his writings that Burns was in love with Margaret Chalmers. In a sisterly way Margaret was good for Burns and it is clear that he felt at ease in her company. His letters to her are amongst his best and she appears to have had a refining influence upon the poet.

During November 1787, Burns sent two love songs to Margaret Chalmers. The first one, *Where braving angry Winter's storms,* appeared in the *Scots Musical Museum* in 1788 to the tune Niel Gow's *Lamentation for Abercairney.*

> Where braving angry Winter's storms
> The lofty Ochils rise,
> For in their shade, my Peggy's charms
> First blest my wandering eyes.
>
> As one who by thy savage stream
> A lonely gem surveys
> Astonish'd doubly marks its beam
> With art' most polished blaze.

Blest be the wild, sequestered glade
And blest the day and hour,
Where Peggy's charms I first survey'd,
When first I felt their pow'r.

The tyrant Death with grim controul
May seize my fleeting breath,
But tearing Peggy from my soul
Must be a stronger death.

When Burns sent Margaret Chalmers the verses for a second song *My Peggy's Charms,* she raised objections to the publication of them. In a letter of reply, Burns pointed out:

I just now have read yours. The poetic compliments I pay cannot be misunderstood. They are neither of them so particular as to point you out to the world at large: and the circle of your acquaintances will allow all I have said. Besides I have complimented you chiefly, almost solely, on your mental charms. Shall I be plain with you? I will; so look to it. Personal attraction, madam, you have much above par; wit, understanding and worth, you possess in the first class. This is a cursed flat way of telling you these truths, but let me hear no more of your timidity.

My Peggy's face, my Peggy's form
The frost of hermit Age might warm.
My Peggy's worth, my Peggy's mind
Might charm the first of human kind.

I love my Peggy's angel air,
Her face so truly heavenly fair,

Her native grace so void of art:
But I adore my Peggy's heart.

The lily's hue, the rose's dye,
The kindling lustre of an eye -
Who but owns their magic sway?
Who but knows they all decay?

The tender thrill, the pitying tear,
The generous purpose, nobly dear,
The gentle look that Rage disarms —
These are all Immortal charms.

It is widely believed that Peggy Chalmers was the girl that Burns had really wanted to marry and long after Burns died she told Thomas Campbell, another poet, that Burns had proposed to her but that she had gently turned him down. She did not give any reasons but it is probable that she was already secretly engaged to Lewis Hay, one of the partners of the Edinburgh banking house of Sir William Forbes, J. Hunter & Co. There is some evidence to support this theory for, on January 17th, 1787, Burns wrote to Gavin Hamilton that he had met a Lothian farmer's daughter whom he had almost persuaded to accompany him to the west country. Thus the reason for Burns's second visit to Harvieston may well have been to further woo the undecided Peggy.

It is certainly worth considering what his life might have been with her as she was a woman of charm, intelligence and literary taste who could also sing and play the piano.

Possibly, like many of the ladies whom Burns met, Peggy Chalmers was in a class above him. Burns was never known to be on sexual terms with women of a better class than himself or with any woman who was his mental equal – although some might argue that Agnes MacLehose (Clarinda,) who he was to meet in the December of that year, was an exception.

During his tours he was made welcome as something of a literary wonder at the grand homes he visited and was allowed to talk freely with the pretty daughters. However, he felt that he was always being kept in his place. Unfortunately, he sometimes forgot his station and tried to treat these genteel young ladies as though they were knickerless country lassies. More than once he went too far and the young lady, as once expressed by Burns, flew off in a tangent of female dignity and reserve. He later told Clarinda that he was frustrated by this at both a psychological and physical level.

Shortly before his death in 1796, Burns sent the following verses for a song, *Fairest Maid on Devon Banks,* to George Thomson for his *Select Collection of Scottish Airs*. This song, so reminiscent of the days at Harviestoun in the Devon valley, was his last and the fairest maid of the song is generally believed to be Peggy Chalmers as she and Burns still remained good but platonic friends after her marriage to Lewis Hay.

However, there is a school of thought that it may have been inspired by the day Burns spent in the company of Charlotte Hamilton during his solo visit in September 1787.

Fairest maid on Devon banks,
Crystal Devon, winding Devon,
Wilt thou lay that frown aside,
And smile as thou wert wont to do.

Full well thou knowest I love thee dear,
Couldst thou to malice lend an ear!
O did not Love exclaim, 'Forbear',
'Nor use a faithful lover so'.

Then come, thou fairest of the fair,
Those wanton smiles O let me share;
And by thy beauteous self I swear,
No love but thine my heart shall know.

Perhaps we shall never know to which girl the song was intended but we do know that an estrangement occurred between Burns and Charlotte Hamilton and that she burnt all the letters which had passed between her and the poet and also many of Peggy's letters. The words of the song do appear to suggest unrequited love.

Although things had not worked out as planned for Burns at Harviestoun, it was a different story for his travelling companion, Dr James Adair, who had now fallen in love with Charlotte Hamilton. Adair decided to remain at Harviestoun to pursue his courtship of Charlotte leaving Burns to continue alone on his intended visits to James Ramsay, the laird of Ochtertyre in the parish of Kincardine Menteith, near Stirling.

Burns wrote of Ramsay as a man to whose words I cannot do justice and Ramsay later recalled the impression that the poet had made on him:

Harviestoun Castle
(demolished 1970)

I have been in the company of many men of genius, some of them poets; but I never witnessed such flashes of intellectual brightness as from him, the impulse of the moment, sparks of celestial fire! I was never more delighted than with his company, two days tete-a-tete on this occasion. In a mixed company I should have made little of him.

Following this visit to James Ramsay, whom he hoped to visit again on his way back to Harviestoun to meet up with Adair, Burns then headed back into Perthshire to another Ochtertyre, near Crieff, where he stayed for several days. Sir William Murray of the Ochtertyre at Crieff had been one of the guests at Blair Castle during Burns's stay there in September and was a cousin of Robert Graham of Fintry who had become a close friend of the poet.

By October 8th, Burns was exceedingly comfortably situated and neither oppressed by ceremony nor mortified by neglect at Sir William's. His hostess, Lady Augusta, was 'a most engaging woman, and very happy in her family, which makes one's outgoings and incomings very agreeable'

During his stay at Ochtertyre he wrote he wrote the poem *On scaring some Water-fowl in Loch Turit, a wild scene among the Hills of Oughtertyre* which were in his own words 'the production of a solitary forenoon's walk from Oughtertyre House'. The poet was surely no mean walker!

> Why, ye tenants of the lake,
> For me your wat'ry haunt forsake?
> Tell me, fellow creatures, why
> At my presence thus you fly?
> Why disturb your social joys,
> Parent, filial, kindred ties? -
> Common friend to you and me,
> Natures gifts to all are free:
> Peaceful keep your dimpling wave,
> Busy feed, or wanton lave;
> Or, beneath the sheltering rock,
> Bide the surging billow's shock.
>
> Conscious, blushing for our race,
> Soon, too soon, your fears I trace.

Man, your proud, usurping foe,
Would be lord of all below;
Plumes himself in freedom's pride,
Tyrant stern to all beside.

The eagle from the cliffy brow,
Marking you his prey below.
In his breast no pity dwells,
Strong necessity compels;
But Man, to whom alone is giv'n
A ray direct from pitying Heav'n,
Glories in his heart humane –
And creatures for his pleasure slain!

In these savage, liquid plains,
Only known to wand'ring swains,
Where the mossy riv'let strays
Far from human haunts and ways,
All on Nature you depend,
And life's poor season peaceful spend.

Or, if Man's superior might
Dare invade your native right.
On the lofty ether borne,
Man with all his powers you scorn;
Swiftly seek, on clanging wings,
Other lakes, and other springs;
And the foe you cannot brave,
Scorn at least to be his slave.

At that time, there were no better known Perthshire families than the Murrays of Ochtertyre and the Murrays of Lintrose near Coupar Angus. Euphemia Murray, a beautiful eighteen-year-old daughter of one of the latter families and known as 'The Flower of Strathmore' was

Loch Turret

visiting her cousins, the Murrays of Ochtertyre, at the same time as Burns. She was later to recall how Burns recited the poem, *On Scaring the Wildfowl,* one evening after supper, and that he gave the concluding lines with the greatest possible vigour.

Burns was smitten by her beauty and grace and in an attempt to woo her, Burns wrote 'Song – composed at Auchtertyre on Miss Euphemia Murray of Lentrose' which he titled *The Flower of Strathmore* and was set to an old tune *Andro an' his Cutty Gun*. According to tradition, Euphemia Murray was not impressed by Burns's tribute to her. It is also believed

Euphemia Murray

~77~

that his first sighting of Miss Murray on the banks of the River Earn inspired Burns to write the verses of *Blythe Was She*.

> Blythe, blythe and merry was she,
> Blythe was she but and ben,
> Blythe by the banks of Earn,
> And blythe in Glenturit glen.
>
> By Oughtertyre grows the aik,
> On Yarrow banks the birken shaw;
> But Phemie was a bonier lass
> Than braes o' Yarrow ever saw.
>
> Her looks were like a flow'r in May,
> Her smile was like a simmer morn.
> She tripped by the banks o' Earn
> As light's a bird upon the thorn.
>
> Her bonie face it was as meek
> As onie lamb upon a lea.
> The evening sun was ne'er sae sweet
> As was the blink o Phemie's e'e.
>
> The Highland hills I've wandered wide,
> As o'er the Lowlands I hae been.
> But Phemie was the blythest lass
> That ever trod the dewy green.

Seven years after her meeting with Burns, Euphemia Murray married the Hon. David Smythe of Methven Castle near Perth, who was one of the senators of the College of Justice. Although she was always disinclined to speak of her meeting with the poet, it is interesting to read the following words from *Perthshire in Bygone Days* which was written in 1879 by the Perth historian and writer Peter R Drummond who lived at Ellengowan near Almondbank near Methven Castle.

> It was my good fortune to meet in after life with 'The Beauty of Strathmore' and I confess having tried covertly to conjure up visions of the poet and the lady strolling about the braes of Auchtertyre — she listening to conversation that never failed to fascinate, and he basking in rays to which his heart ever turned. The lady's amiable and kind-hearted sister, now some years deceased, told me some charming reminiscences of Burns — how she met him at Sir James Hunter Blair's, 'when she was young and perhaps rather handsome', and how she blushed and shrank from the gaze that followed her on being placed next to the poet, and of his manly and easy bearing and how his eyes 'glowed like live coals when his own songs were sung'.
>
> This visit to Auchtertyre has always welled up in my mind as the beauty spot of the poet's life. Away up in Glenturrit, young, healthful and prosperous, in company with the best and fairest of the land, set down to dinner on the right hand of the handsome and accomplished daughter of the great Earl of Cromarty, a Jacobite grafted into a Whig family, the group formed a subject of much interest to such a man as Robert Burns.

CHAPTER FIVE

Back in Edinburgh, the later years and the legacy

After leaving Perthshire for the final time, Burns returned to Harviestoun on October 20th to be reunited with James Adair who had, in the poet's absence, become engaged to be married to Charlotte Hamilton.

After Charlotte's marriage to Adair two years later, Burns sent the song, *The Banks of the Devon,* to George Thomson with the accompanying note:

These verses were composed on a charming girl, a Miss Charlotte Hamilton, who is now married to Jas. McKitrick Adair, Esquire, Physician. She is sister of my worthy friend Gavin Hamilton.

The song was set to a Gaelic melody, *Bhannerach dhon na chri,* which Burns had noted down during his visit to Inverness.

How pleasant the banks of the clear winding Devon,
With green spreading bushes and flow'rs blooming fair!
But the boniest flow'r on the banks of the Devon
Was once a sweet bud on the braes of the Ayr.

Mild be the sun on this sweet blushing flower,
In the gay rosy morn, as it bathes in the dew!
And gentle the fall of the soft vernal shower,
That steals on the evening each leaf to renew!

O, spare the dear blossom, ye orient breezes,
With chill, hoary wing as ye usher the dawn!
And far be thou distant, thou reptile that seizes
The verdure and pride of the garden or lawn!

> Let Bourbon exult in his gay gilded lilies,
> And England triumphant display her proud rose!
> A fairer than either adorns the green valleys,
> Where Devon, sweet Devon, meandering flows.

It is said that on the visit to Harviestoun earlier that month, that while Burns had disappointed the house party by showing insufficient appreciation of the local scenery, he had relished an incident which Adair described:

A visit to Mrs Bruce of Clackmannan, a lady above ninety, the lineal descendant of that race which gave the Scottish throne its brightest ornament, interested his feelings more powerfully. This venerable dame, with characteristical dignity, informed me, on my observing that I believed she was descended from the family of Robert Bruce, that Robert Bruce was sprung from her family. Though almost deprived of speech by a paralytic affection, she preserved her hospitality and urbanity. She was in possession of the hero's helmet and two-handed sword, with which she conferred on Burns and myself the honour of Knighthood, remarking that she had a better right to confer the title than some people.

During their journey back to Edinburgh, the two men visited Dunfermline Abbey where, according to Adair: 'In the courtyard, two broad flag-stones mark the grave of Robert Bruce, for whose memory Burns had more than common veneration. He knelt and kissed the stone with sacred fervour, and heartily.'

Back in Edinburgh, after crossing the River Forth at Queensferry, Burns planned to leave the city by the end of 1787. However, after a quick trip to Dumfries in November regarding the possible lease of a farm in that area, two events coincided which were to keep him in

Edinburgh and precipitate one of the most famous episodes in his life. He met Agnes McLehose and he wrenched his knee so badly that he could not leave his room for a month or travel for ten weeks.

The accident on December 8th, caused by a drunken coachman, also led to Burns finally securing an appointment in the Excise. One of the doctors, Alexander Wood, learnt that Burns really wanted the appointment and set wheels in motion to get it for him. The person reponsible for securing it was Robert Graham of Fintry who Burns had met at Blair Castle and who was now a member of the Scottish Board of Excise.

On December 4th, Burns met and then entered into what seems to have been a platonic dalliance with Agnes (Nancy) McLehose, a woman of some social standing, who was herself in an ambiguous social situation – her husband having been in Jamaica for some time. For the first few weeks, due to Burns being incapacitated by the accident, the relationship stimulated a correspondence in which Burns and Mrs McLehose styled themselves Sylvander and Clarinda. They were certainly attracted to each other but, whatever its true nature, it is doubtful if their love was ever consummated. However, there is certainly no doubt whatsoever about the nature of the poet`s relationship with Nancy's domestic servant Jenny Clow who bore him a son, Robert Burns Clow, in 1788.

Burns finally left Edinburgh on February 18th , 1788 and, furnished with the sum of about £500 from the Edinburgh collection of his poems, returned to Ayrshire.

The success of his time in Edinburgh was to bring another consequence. The father of Jean Armour, who had earlier refused Burns permission to marry his pregnant daughter, now saw the poet as a suitable son-in-law and relented on his opposition to the marriage.

Robert Burns set up home in Mauchline with Jean and their twins that same month but in June the family moved to the Dumfries area where Burns took a lease on a farm at Ellisland on the banks of the River Nith. However, in common with many eighteenth century farms, the soil at Ellisland was exhausted after years of extensive cultivation and neither crop growing or dairy farming was sustainable. He is quoted as having said that 'the Lord riddled all creation and the riddlings he poured on Ellisland'

In order to provide a living for his family, Burns moved them to the town of Dumfries where he took up the commission which had earlier been offered to him and became an exciseman.

For the next six years Burns found little opportunity for touring Scotland although he became familiar with a large tract of country as his duties as an exciseman entailed almost two hundred miles of horseback riding each week. However one trip of only a few days duration, made from Dumfries with his friend Syme, was notable as having given birth to that great battle song of all time – *Scots Wha Hae*.

Unfortunately, following a lengthy period of ill health, Burns died on 21st July, 1796 – only nine years after his Highland tour.

It is no exaggeration to describe Robert Burns as a tourist as he was unquestionably one of the most travelled men of his day. There are people of the present day who, with ever so many more opportunities, are much less acquainted with their native country. Burns's tours and in particular his Highland Tour, had a profound influence on him and some of that influence has been roughly indicated in this book.

It is quite possible that he would still have risen to the great height of being Scotland's National Bard without travelling beyond the bounds of his native Ayrshire. But it is good to think that a man who knew so well the hearts of the people of Scotland and helped preserve her language and traditions and retain her identity, also knew its rivers, mountains, glens and the places chiefly renowned in the national history.

SELECT BIBLIOGRAPHY AND SOURCES OF INFORMATION

Barke, James, *The Wonder of All the Gay World* (1949. London. Collins).

Brown, Raymond Lamont, *Robert Burns's Tours of the Highlands and Stirlingshire 1787* (1973. Ipswich. The Boydell Press).

Burns Chronicle, The, (volumes for 1904, 1957, 2001. Kilmarnock. The Robert Burns World Federation).

Drummond, P R, *Perthshire in Bygone Days* (1879. London. Whittingham).

Fitzhugh, Robert T, *Robert Burns the Man and the Poet* (1970. Boston, USA. Houghton Mifflin Company).

Gilfillan, Rev. George, *The National Burns* (London, Glasgow, Edinburgh. William Mackenzie).

Haynes, Nick, *Perth & Kinross. An illustrated architectural guide* (2000. Edinburgh. The Rutland Press).

Jack, J W , *Scott's View from the Wicks of Baiglie* (1933. Perth. Milne, Tannahill & Methven).

Lindsay, Maurice, *The Burns Encylopaedia* (1959, 1970. London. Hutchinson)

Mackay, James A (ed.), *The Complete Poetical Works of Robert Burns* (1986. Ayr. Alloway Publishing).

Mackay, James A (ed.), *The Complete Letters of Robert Burns* (1987. Ayr. Alloway Publishing).

Melville, Lawrence, *The Fair Land of Gowrie* (1939. Coupar Angus. William Culross & Son Ltd.)

Paton, Donald N M, *'Twixt Castle and Mart* (2005. Perth. Perth & Kinross Libraries).

Tranter, Nigel, *The Heartland. Clackmannanshire, Perthshire and Stirlingshire* (1971. London. Hodder and Stoughton Limited).

Newspapers and Magazines:

The Perthshire Advertiser; The Courier and Advertiser; The Scots Magazine..

Websites:

The Robert Burns World Federation. The Poetry Foundation. Georgian Edinburgh. Dollar Museum. Electric Scotland. The Perth Burns Club.

INDEX

A Highland Welcome 11, 56
Aberfeldy 34, 36-39
Aberuchil 26, 29
Adair, James 74, 69, 80
Address to Beezlebub 33
Address to the Woodlark 42
Allan Water 26-27
Almondbank 79
Amang the Trees 43
Amulree 31
An ye had been whare I hae been 46
Andro an' his Cutty Gun 78
Ardoch camp 26
Armour, Jean 22, 82
Auchtertyre 26, 29, 77, 79
Balgowan 52, 63-64
Bannockburn 24
Belches, Wilhelmina 64
Benny Water 48
Bessy Bell and Mary Gray 62
Bhannerach dhon na chri 80
Birnam Hill 39-40
Blair Atholl 7, 44, 50, 54-55, 62
Blair Castle 7, 48, 50-51, 54, 68, 75, 82
Blythe Was She 78
Brodie, William 18
Bruar Water 49, 5- 52, 54-55
Bryce, Rev Alex 64
Burns Supper. 10
Burns, Robert 1, 3-12, 17-19, 21-26, 29-39, 41-52, 54-75, 77-80,
By Allan Stream. 27
Campbell, John 33
Campbell, Thomas 72
Carse of Gowrie 58
Castle Menzies 34, 36, 38
Chalmers, Margaret 24, 25, 70-73
Clow, Jenny 82

Comrie 26, 28-29
Corsiehill 58, 62
Covenanters 45-46
Creech, William 18-19, 68
Crieff 7, 26, 29, 50, 67, 75
Croft Moraig stone circle 34, 36
Croom's Tavern 60-62
Culloden 46, 57-58
Cunningham, James 17, 23
Dalnacardoch 56
Dalrymple, James 17
Dalwhinnie 55, 56
Dr Jekyll and Mr Hyde 18
Drummond Castle 29
Duchess of Gordon 19
Duke of Atholl 39, 47, 52, 55
Dumfries 44, 52, 81, 83
Dunkeld 7, 34, 38, 40, 67
Edinburgh 17-19, 21, 22, 25, 47, 59-61, 64, 67-69, 72, 80-82, 68-69
Epigram on Rough Roads 11
Episcopalians 46
Erskine, David Stewart 20
Evelick Castle 59
Failte na miosg 57
Fairest Maid on Devon Banks 73
Falls of Acharn 33, 36
Falls of Moness 36
Ferguson, Adam 7, 19
Fingask House 58
Forbes, Sir William 72
Forteviot 64
Glen Quaich 31
Glenalmond 30
Glenlyon House 34-35, 38
Gow, Niel 7, 38, 41, 44-45, 70
Gowrie House, 62
Graham, Robert 7 51, 68, 75, 82

Graham, Thomas 52
Grant, Sir James 68
Grantully 34
Hamilton, Charlotte 70, 73-74, 80
Hamilton, Gavin 25, 72, 80
Harviestoun 24-26, 70, 73-75, 80-81
Harviestoun Castle 24-25, 70, 74
Hay, Lewis. 73
Hermit's Cave 33-34, 36
Hermitage 38
Hey ca' thro' 66
Inver 35, 38-39, 41, 44
Invercauld Reel 42
Invermay House 64-65
Jacobites 45-46, 58, 79
James Graham of Claverhouse 45
Johnson, James 18
Kenmore 32, 33-35
Kenmore Inn 11, 32
Killiecrankie 11, 45-47, 59
Kinross 62, 65-68
Kinross Jolly Beggars Burns Club 10, 67
Lamentation for Abercairney 70
Leezie Lindsay 60
Loch Fruoch 30
Loch Garrie 55
Loch Leven 66
Loch Tay 32, 35
Loch Tummel 49
Locherrochside 42
Logierait 7, 19, 39, 41
Lord Glencairn 18
Malloch, William 64
Marquis of Tullibardine 47
Mary Queen of Scots 66
McPherson, James 30, 37
Meall A'Choire Chreagaich 32
Menzies, Sir John 36
Methven Castle 79

Monymusk 42
Murray, Sir William 7, 29, 49-50, 75
Murrayshall Hill 52
Muthill 29
My Love Is Like a Red, Red Rose 7, 42
My Peggy's Charms 71
National Galleries Scotland 6
National Trust Scotland 6
Nicol, William 11, 21-22, 24, 26, 29, 31, 35, 44, 50-52, 56, 58, 60, 65, 69-70
Ochil Hills 65
Ochtertyre 7, 29, 50, 63-64, 74-75, 77
Ochtertyre House 29, 64
On Scaring the Wild-fowl 75, 77
Ossian 30-31, 38-39, 68
Ossian's stone 30, 31
Perth 4-5, 7, 9-10, 29, 32, 47, 52, 58, 60-63, 79, 68-69
Perth Burns Club 4-5, 10
Poems, Chiefly in the Scottish Dialect 17
Purdie, David 3, 6
Raeburn, Sir Henry 45
Rait 58
Richmond, John 17
River Allan 26, 28
River Almond 30, 62
River Braan 39, 41
River Earn 28-29, 78
River Garry 46, 56
River Lyon 36
River May 64
River Tay. 36
River Tilt 48, 50
River Tummel 44
Rothiemurchie 55-56
Scone Palace 62
Scots Musical Museum 18, 21, 59, 70
Scots Wha Hae 83
Scott, Sir Walter 64

~87~

Scottish Enlightenment 17
Smythe, David 79
Stewart, Alexander 39
Stewart, Dugald 18
Strathallan, 29
Stuarts 46
Tait, John 24-25
Tam o' Shanter 10
Taymouth Castle 33
The Banks of the Devon 80
The Birks of Aberfeldy 11, 36-37,
    39
The Birks of Invermay 64
The Flower of Strathmore 77
The Humble Petition of Bruar Water 11
The Merry Muses 18
Thomson, George 27, 42, 73, 80
Threipland, Sir Stewart 58
Townsend, Charles 30
Tullochgorum 42
Viscount Dundee 45-46, 59
Wade`s Bridge 36
Walker, Josiah   7, 45, 47, 49-52,
    54, 63
Where braving angry Winter's storms 70
Whiteford, Sir John 17
Yon Wild Mossy Mountains 59

Also by Donald N M Paton
in Rymour Books

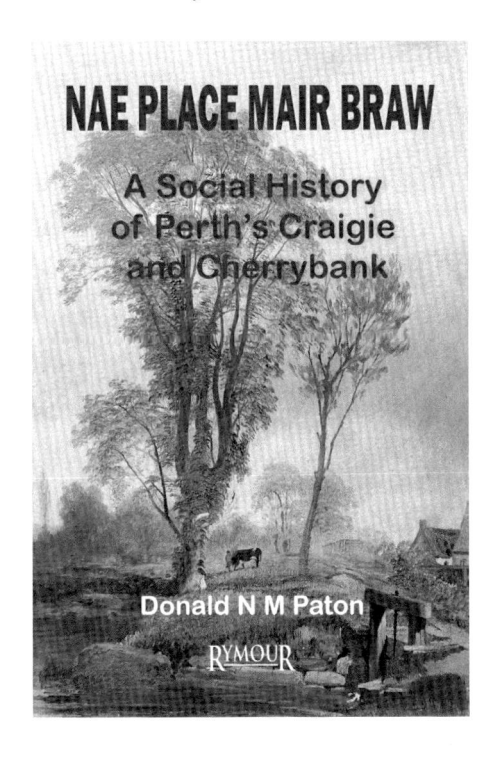

NAE PLACE MAIR BRAW

A Social History of Perth's Craigie and Cherrybank

Donald N M Paton

RYMOUR